ever wonder?
why we do it?

To all the friends I have
sailed with, with fond
memories.

ever wonder?
why we do it
mike peyton

ADLARD COLES NAUTICAL
LONDON

Published by Adlard Coles Nautical
an imprint of A & C Black Publishers Ltd
38 Soho Square, London, W1D 3HB
www.adlardcoles.com

First edition 2007

ISBN 978-0-7136-8291-5

A CIP catalogue record for this book is available from the British Library.

This book is produced using paper that is made from wood grown in managed,
sustainable forests. It is natural, renewable and recyclable. The logging and
manufacturing processes conform to the environmental regulations of the country
of origin.

Typeset in 11/14.5pt Celeste Regular by Falcon Oast Graphic Art Ltd.
Printed and bound in Singapore by Star Standard.

Contents

Foreword

Drawing on experience

One of the delights of working at *Yachting Monthly* magazine is opening an envelope each month from which spill Mike Peyton's colourful cartoons. He is best known for his illustrations for The Confessional, where readers own up in print to their most embarrassing sailing moments.

It would probably make Mike shudder to be called 'an institution in yachting', but that's what he is – and a much loved one, too. His cartoons and occasional articles have graced the pages of our magazine, and others, for more than 35 years, causing ripples of laughter from the Thames Estuary to Tahiti. Mike has seen off more editors than any other contributor in our 101-year history. Yet he remains a modest, almost shy man, unaware of the esteem in which he is held.

Here is a man who can literally draw on his experiences. Mike's mischievous sense of satire is informed by his own inimitable exploits on the water in a succession of odd craft. After studying at Manchester Art School, he bought a 12ft canvas sailing canoe from a man in a Richmond pub. He worked his way down the River Thames sleeping on moored barges and remembers frying breakfast on a primus stove under the shadow of Big Ben. Eventually, he reached salt water and learned to cope with tides and how to reef sails the hard way. His own first proper boat was 24ft *Vagrant*, so-called 'because she had no visible means of support.'

In the primeval East Coast mud, Mike discovered a whole emerging sub-species of the yachting world. Perhaps because yachting in those days was a serious business – sailors wore peaked caps and ensigns were lowered at sunset – Mike felt impelled to stick a pin in the balloon of sailing snobbery and pomposity.

With a few strokes of his pen and a few squiggly lines – though, of course, there's far more to it than that! – Mike's down-to-earth sense of humour transports you to the heart and soul of sailing dilemmas. For me, there's no other sailing cartoonist in the world who can match his elegant, economical wit and wisdom. Mike's humour may be merciless, but it's also gentle rather than vulgar, brash or cruel. To an editor Mike Peyton is a gift and a joy.

He is not only a superb draughtsman, but he also has a winning way with words, whether it's a double-entendre, a clever punch line, headline or caption. He is also an exceptional raconteur, as anyone who has sat below in the cosy saloon of *Touchstone*, his current boat, with the coal stove glowing, can testify after listening to his yarns.

Mike has been a unique commentator on the sailing scene for more than 50 years. He tells me he gets his best cartoon ideas sitting in the bath. Perhaps it's the catalyst of being surrounded by water instead of East Coast mud!

Meanwhile, at the tender age of 86, he goes sailing in his favourite Essex creeks and swatchways whenever wind and weather permit – he still goes skiing, too! But these days he tries to avoid cartoon situations . . . mostly with success!

Paul Gelder
Editor of Yachting Monthly *magazine*

Chapter 1

Maiden voyage

My sailing experience had been pretty near minimal when I bought my first cruising boat, on an impulse. I had the loan of a heavy, eight foot, flat-bottomed, gunter rigged dinghy for about a month and in her I discovered the joys of running before the wind, tempered only by the knowledge that the further I ran the further I would have to row back. On the basis of these experiences having, in a manner of speaking, discovered the beginning of the trail to the Holy Grail, I set off to hire a cruising boat for a week's holiday – and fell by the wayside. As I've said, it was an impulse buy, and there I was, an instant yachtsman. And, since it took almost all of our savings, almost an instant bachelor.

However, as we had signed up for better or for worse we survived, me getting the better in this case.

The boat I now owned had, in a sense, been bought out of 'trade'. She had been what was known as a penny sick, taking holidaymakers from Southend beach to the end of the pier and back. She was a 7.3m x 2.5m x 0.5m (24ft x 8ft 6ins x 1ft 6ins) gaff sloop rigged centre-boarder. Originally an open boat, her topsides had been built up by her previous owner to give sitting headroom and her decks were covered with thick red lino. She had a large cockpit, had been used as a floating caravan, and had never sailed beyond Burnham. Now, with all honesty, I can describe her as a box with a pointed end, but then no feeble words of mine would have been adequate enough to describe what I thought of her. I used to sit on the seawall just looking at her.

On our first sail I doubt if any boat ever went to sea with such a crew of amateurs on board. In the first place we had no intention of going to sea when we set off, as the sum total of our combined experience was me being on the delivery trip, all of three miles down the river with the previous owner on board, and my running-cum-rowing outings. The rest of the crew were Tommy, a neighbour and ex-army friend, who had seen the sea before and Gabor, a Hungarian refugee, who hadn't.

We also had on board, by proxy in a manner of speaking, one Peter Heaton, in my eyes one of the finest and most underestimated authors these Islands have produced. He was the author of an invaluable Penguin paperback called *Sailing,* and no tablets of stone were ever studied with such reverence and dedication as was that book. Gabor had his new English Hungarian Dictionary – we flipped through them in unison, both at about the same level of competence. The plan was simply to sail down the River Crouch and sail back. But sailing being what it is, it didn't work out like that.

On that distant halcyon day when we set sail from the upper reaches of the Crouch, Gabor had sole charge of the boathook with a roving commission. Tommy and I had the rest of the boat and Peter Heaton had pride of place on the engine box; on call as one might say. The boat actually had an engine, an 8hp Brooke Marine, but it wasn't working. However this worried me not, as the accepted advice of the time was that one should eschew engines until one was competent enough to handle one's boat under sail. I'm very good at eschewing. It's so simple. So I eschewed. I was to regret it later.

We ran down the Crouch with a fresh south-westerly behind us and the tide under us in a state of bliss. With hindsight I realise the novelty of it all for Gabor must have been out of this world. But when at Shore Ends, with open sea before us, I tried to return and found I couldn't. The wind that had wafted us down, now that we were trying to go against it, went up considerably in strength and I literally couldn't control the boat. I found out later she had once been cutter rigged with a bowsprit and now without the bowsprit and the jib she was completely unbalanced. I didn't

PEYTON

know enough to reef the main to redress this, or have enough sense to anchor and wait for the tide to turn. The engine I had eschewed and my normal answer to this problem, rowing, were both out of the question. And in our hour of need Mr Heaton deserted us, slipping from his place of honour on the engine box into the bilges and was pulp before we could spare the time to rescue him. We did the only thing we knew how to: we ran before it.

Hugging the coast, as we wanted to keep as close to the land as we could, we noticed that there was no doubt the blue skies which we had started under were now definitely greyer. Gabor, losing all his early enthusiasm, was as sick as a dog in this run up the coast with the wind getting stronger all the time. He blew up the lilo which was to have been his bed and clutched it like a comfort blanket. From his body language you didn't have to understand Hungarian to know what he was thinking. Before his dictionary had gone the way of Mr Heaton, I had seen him flipping feverishly through the pages before he came out with a classic bit of English understatement. 'Puddle! Puddle!' pointing into the cabin, I got the shock of my life when I looked in. It seemed to be full of water sloshing around, with the floorboards awash and everything that could float floating, and what couldn't sodden. Every time the boat hit a wave the centreboard case seemed to grow two white ears as water shot out of where the centreboard bolt was. I started pumping.

We had another panic when Tommy drew my attention to some seagulls standing up ahead of us. We sheered off – this was my initiation into the hazards of the ochre seas of the Thames estuary. In efforts to keep close to land we had finally ended up hard on the wind. We were learning, but as the shore ran off to the west we could no longer stay with it. We weren't unduly worried as the north shore was ahead of us and stretched out on both sides, impossible to miss. We bucketed on across the lonely Blackwater.

Ultimately there came a time when it seemed we would hit the saltings, though this would have suited Gabor. For my part, while pleased to be so close to terra firma, I didn't want to be that close, so I scrambled along the deck, unlashed the anchor and flung it over the side. The result was almost as if we had hit a brick wall and only a frantic grab at the forestay stopped me following it into the sea. I had never realised anchors were so efficient. We scrambled the sails down and almost relaxed for the first time since we'd left. Was it only a few short hours ago we'd set off? It seemed like a lifetime. Tommy, standing in the bilges, reverted to the old ways that had seen us through difficult times in the past – when in doubt brew up, so he lit the primus.

Rested and refreshed, we now had an objective – simply to reach the anchorage of the boats whose masts we could see over the saltings. It was when we attempted to pull up the anchor we found out why we had been brought up all standing. By some million to one chance as the anchor had gone down it had hooked itself in a huge wire cable. As Gabor weighed up his chances of reaching the saltings on his lilo Tommy and I wrestled with the problem of freeing ourselves from this cable which, by much effort and risk, we had managed to get up from the sea bed and could now see just below the surface. Fortunately Mr Heaton (in a manner of speaking) was still with us. Impressed on my memory was the fact that this very problem had all been covered in the chapter titled Anchoring. All dinghies in those days carried dinghy anchors. Our dinghy was no exception so, all according to The Book, we hooked the cable with the dinghy anchor and, after taking the strain on it, released the main anchor. Waiting until we were pointing in the desired direction we tripped the dinghy anchor and went bucketing off again. When we were in the vicinity of the moored boats in what I now realise was Mersea Quarters, I flung the anchor out again and we automatically braced ourselves for the brick wall bit, but this time nothing happened. In fact just the opposite – we were rapidly being blown down on some moored boats. The adrenalin was rising again when the anchor fouled a mooring and we swung head to wind and stopped.

Our Maiden Voyage was over. Tommy, practical as ever, took the cover off the engine. 'We should have done this first,' he said. Gabor, I later found out, had started composing a letter in his mind to the High Commissioner of Australia wanting confirmation that if he did go to Australia on that assisted passage could he travel by air? If not count him out.

But I was on cloud nine, give or take a few things such as being twenty odd miles from where I had planned to be, and, forgetting the initial shock of seeing the floorboards floating and seagulls standing where they should have floated, I knew without a doubt I had arrived.

'I'll see you later. I made a promise out there –
I'm going to church.'

Chapter 2

Messing about with boats

We had just finished lunch, my wife and I, when the phone rang. 'It's the yard here. The engineer wants to know what's the trouble with your engine?'

'Hang on. I'll come down.' (I live close to the yard.)

I told my wife, who replied, 'Don't forget, Vic and Lena are coming at eight for a meal.'

'Don't be ridiculous,' said I, huffily. 'It's not two o'clock yet.'

'I'm not being ridiculous. I am simply reminding you that Vic and Lena are coming over at eight o'clock.'

I drove the couple of miles to the yard, in a manner of speaking, on my high horse. I rowed Dick the engineer down to the boat on the ebb tide. The sun was shining and I thought, 'What more pleasant way to spend a couple of hours mid-week than pottering on the boat?' On board, Dick made his diagnosis.

'It looks as if that dog has jammed in the starter motor. We'll have it off.'

And so we started. We moved the batteries on to the cabin sole, and as I moved the second one I knocked the box of tools over. All the tools spilled out and one, one tool only, went into the bilges, a small moveable.

Dick nodded morosely. 'That's it.'

'It's fired.'

I put the batteries on a bunk and pulled up the boards.

`We could do with a small tommy bar. Have you got one?'

I have and I keep it under the bunk. I moved the batteries again, and it wasn't the starter motor.

`It's inside. I can probably fix it from behind.'

Behind is also below the cockpit. Together we started on taking up the cockpit floor. Screw-heads broke off; the quarter-round broke. Dick finally disappeared down the hole. He was down a long time, and quiet; ominously quiet. He emerged.

`I still can't get at it. We'll have to move the engine forward.'

We disconnected holding-down bolts, fuel line, water, throttle, exhaust, drive. Floor boards up, batteries on forward bunk, oil and grease marks everywhere. We moved the engine forward, down the hole, up from the hole, not far enough. More levering, more straining, more oil, more grease, more curses, back down the hole, up from the hole, won't go any further, sump in the way. We'll have to lift. Look up at the open hatch, some four by four foot across.

`Unship the mainsail. I have some four by four.'

I went to get the four by four. It was forward under the bunk with batteries on top. Restraining myself from manhandling them through the forehatch and dropping them over the side, I transferred them to the port bunk and all the rest of the gear that was with them, and got the four by four.

On to the next problem: make slings under engine, transfer mainsheet, wrong lead, take off, reverse, replace choc-o-bloc. Wants raising, not enough height. More four by four. No four by four. Use bunk-boards. It takes longer to do than write. Still not high enough. I remembered the old service adage – when in doubt, brew up – so I lit the stove and put the kettle on. Sitting on the cross-members in the midst of the chaos with our feet in the bilges, we ruminated, while the engine squatted there, dominating the saloon like some vast armoured creature halfway out of its black lair.

It was obvious that what we had to do was to get the boat alongside the stage and use the crane. We had no engine or sails, as the main sheet now had the engine on it. The work boat was moored up for the night and the yard men gone home. In the gathering gloom I got out a line to tow the boat from the dinghy. I rowed off and took the strain. Dick cast off and it started to rain. We had our little crises, inevitable manoeuvring a 33ft boat through crowded moorings with a good tide running, but we managed –

until we ran aground barely twenty feet from the landing and the crane. I made my line fast ashore and rowed back. We would just have to wait for water.

'I'm sorry,' Dick said, 'I'll just have to leave you to it. I'm taking the wife out.'

I rowed him ashore, returned on board and went below to shelter from the rain. Getting below was an operation in itself, squeezing under the lash-up of a hoist we had made over the engine. Once below, it was lethal, absolute chaos. The floorboards were up and anything that you could put a foot on was covered in oil or grease. Gear and tools, warps and wood were everywhere. It seemed as if everything that could be moved on the boat had been moved, and it was black as pitch. With no lights I pulled out the Tilley lamp. It was empty. I knew where the paraffin was – where it always was – forward under the port bunk, the one with the batteries on. By the time I had got the paraffin and lit the lamp there was enough water to warp the boat alongside the stage. I went through the drill in the darkness: bowline, stern-line, head warp, stern warp, springs, unshackle the main halyard for masthead line, fenders over the side and planks. All I had to do was turn out the Tilley lamp and go home. I jumped into the cockpit. In mid-air I remembered that it no longer had a floor.

If anyone else had been there they would have said, 'Gosh, you were lucky!' And I suppose I was but, straddling that cross-member, I didn't think so then. I climbed painfully back onto the bridgedeck and looked below through the tangled web of lines and timber. I could have wept at what I saw: it was everything a boat shouldn't be. I left the Tilley to burn itself out and drove home.

If ever a man needed a drink I did. The pub was closing as I arrived. I pressed on, incensed. They do say accidents are caused by bad temper and I can believe it. I screeched round the bend into the lane. Very little traffic uses it by day let alone at night – it was only the quick reactions of the driver of the white Mini which took off into the hedge that prevented the accident there and then. I roared on and stormed into the house.

'Some idiot in a white Mini nearly saw me off!'

'Yes' replied my wife. 'That would be Vic and Lena.'

Then my troubles really started.

'I'll be back immediately.'

'It's your wife. She wants to know if you're enjoying
your silver wedding anniversary.'

'I know you sail to get away from your wife.
But surely she can't be as bad as this?'

Chapter 3

First sail of the season

Frozen water pipes are something one associates with houses, not boats, but that was our problem. We had arrived late because of the icy road conditions, slung our gear and a sack of coal on board, then slithered around the snow-covered deck to cast off the frozen mooring warps.

Now, going down the Blackwater on the ebb, surrounded by ice floes, a mug of hot tea took on a new attraction. It was then we realised we had frozen pipes.

Luck, or the past, was with us. Some years previously I had read about a large American schooner that had ended up as a disaster area because the electrics failed. They couldn't start the engine, hoist the sails, use the anchor or pump water. The lack of water I could identify with, not that I used electricity to pump it, but just in case I had filled a two-gallon water container and stowed it under a quarter berth, and had almost forgotten it.

Their misfortune solved ours. Vintage water it may have been, but not only did we have our tea, but hot water poured down the water pipe put us back on the mains. Judiciously applied, it also freed the frozen cars on the sail track. We were back in business.

January was an inclement month to say the least, but, going down the river – there were six of us aboard *Touchstone* – we had no complaints. A fair tide, a quartering breeze and a long weekend ahead: what more could one want? Even if it was minus four. That night we had Pyefleet Creek to ourselves and, as ever, there was an amazing contrast: a tiny cocoon of warmth, light and comfort in a bitterly cold, inclement world. I awoke and from the glow of the stove I saw it was two o'clock. There was the sound of a boat coming alongside. I shot out of my sleeping bag and stuck my head out of the hatch. Nothing. Had I been imagining it?

No – Richard was also up, and he had heard it too. I shone a torch around, but there was nothing to be seen. Then I looked at the water and found the answer. The noise was ice scraping along the hull as the ebb started.

We both knew that if we wanted to go north we should be making use of this ebb tide and going with it – but we said nothing and a couple of minutes later we were both back in our still-warm sleeping bags. We are keen sailors, but not that fanatically keen.

By the time we had salted the icy decks and were underway the following morning, there was little of the ebb left, and at the bar buoy we had a decision to make: a fair tide and a beat south into the Thames, or a foul tide and a run north to Harwich? The wind was fresh from the south-west, so the wind chill factor decided it for us. We eased out sheets and ran north.

It was a fabulous day for sailing. A brilliant, blue, cloudless sky although even with the wind behind us it was bitterly cold and, with the amount of clothes we were wearing, we looked like a crew of Michelin-tyre men.

The wind eased as we sailed into the Orwell and it was dark before we approached Woolverstone Marina. In the darkness the deserted pontoons seemed to be covered in frozen snow, but it was even more slippery than that – it was bird droppings. For some physical reason, no doubt concerning the cormorant's digestive process, it had not frozen. The first two ashore with the lines almost found this out too late.

Our original intention of going to Woolverstone was to walk back to the Butt and Oyster, but our luck was in. The Royal Harwich Yacht Club was lit up and bustling. It was a big night; the annual dinner of the flag officers and their ladies. I thought that between us we represented the two extremes of yachting clobber, but we were warmly welcomed by the secretary and, having been shown an inconspicuous corner, the saving on walking time was easily re-allocated to drinking time.

The following morning there was a change in the weather – fog. Walton Coastguard station gave two hundred yards of visibility, but to us

'It beats me what they see in it.'

it was dense. But dense enough to stay tied up? At times like this I always think of the story of the two shoe salesmen who were sent off to some remote area of the world. One sent a message to his office saying: 'Returning immediately – no one wears shoes here.' The other sent a message reading: 'Send all the shoes you have – no one wears shoes here.'

Did we look on the fog as a drawback, or the opportunity for some interesting navigation? We chose the latter and decided to go to Mistley, approximately 15 miles away – six miles down the Orwell to Harwich, and about nine miles up the River Stour. Going down the Orwell, it was as if we were sailing blindfolded. In fact, we never saw either bank until we arrived at Mistley.

As a problem, it was interesting, but we were grateful it was not as in pre-Decca days. One may talk of the good old days, but I prefer the comfort of a warm doghouse as against leaning on a shroud and swinging a lead with wet and frozen fingers.

I still consider an echo sounder an amazing bit of user-friendly kit, but I look on my box of navigational feedback as the early mariners must have looked at the stars – magical. We made two rules. One was to keep out of the shipping channel. The second was that the lookout in the bows made the decisions, and only shouted when the helmsman had to turn 90°, to port or starboard.

So we hauled up the radar reflector and set off under engine. We saw three boats. The first was a small boat at anchor with two men fishing from it. They must have heard us coming with apprehension and were probably thinking the same as us – I wonder what pleasure they see in that?

The next was an RNLI RIB and then, still sticking to our plan of keeping out of the channel, I think we sensed before we saw that we had the third ship abeam. It was, we found out later, a small Russian cargo ship and, as it was past Parkestone Quay, it must have been bound for Mistley. It would have had a pilot on board. Our navigational exercise was put on hold, and we followed in its wake.

We passed it as it went alongside the quay by the mill and we crept on to the public quay, where *Touchstone* was recognised. As we closed in, out of the fog came a voice. 'Hello, Mike. We've lost a Russian ship. You haven't seen one coming up?' The greeting was from a friend of mine, a customs officer, and the last time I had seen her was only a few days previously at a Christmas party – drink in hand and wearing a paper hat.

Now it was a clip board and a hard hat. We pointed to where her duty lay and made for the pub, mission accomplished.

It was the ebb tide that got us out of the pub and again we relied on our electronic magic to get us back to Harwich, where we picked up a buoy off Shotley in Harwich Harbour. Throughout the night there was the sound of foghorns and I thought I heard the patter of rain, but over breakfast I was corrected – not rain but the pattering of sanderlings.

We had a keen birdwatcher on board, who said he had never done it from a sleeping bag before, but that is what he had been doing. From his bunk he had the unique opportunity of being able to watch the sanderlings from below, through the perspex of the forehatch, a sort of worm's eye view. There was plenty of guano on deck to back up his sightings. On the credit side the visibility was improving, though Force 6 from the south was forecast.

By the time we had got off Stone Banks, it was clear enough to see Walton pier. The wind was fair and we had about 30 miles to cover with all the tide to come, and the sea to ourselves. What more could half a dozen yachties ask for? It was January the 13th. We'd had a good start to the season by anybody's book.

'In those articles of sailing in winter
they always have cold crisp days.'

'There's nothing I like better than a full gale, a few beers
and being tied to a pontoon listening to Channel 16.'

Chapter 4

So near to heaven; so far from work

As a former charter skipper I can say in all truth that the worst thing about the job is the charterers. And before they start ringing and writing to cancel their bookings I can also say in all truth that the best thing about the job is the charterers. The reason for this ambiguity is as follows. The boat is going well, tide under you, sun on your face, wind on your cheek – you do it because you like sailing. Besides the pleasure of the sail, your mind runs as follows, 'marvellous people these charterers – those three on the foredeck, for instance, call them moorings, insurance and grub; the one at the tiller, diesel, gas and a new pair of oars; those three on the doghouse, twenty percent of the new sail on order; the one below, beer money'. Obviously the sums vary from week to week, but it's bound to be good, bless 'em.

On the other hand, ask me when it's a wet, miserable Friday night, the start of a weekend's charter, a dozen figures floundering around their cars in the mud, someone drops their sleeping bag, someone else steps on it, we've missed the tide, a strong wind is forecast and the faint lights of my friendly pub disappear as we go over the sea wall to a cold wet world, rowing into the darkness. Why do they want to do it? Why do I? Money? If I sold the boat and invested the money I could probably be as well off

financially, and if you costed out the hourly rates of pay, any self-respecting trade unionist would have a stroke before he could shout 'strike'. For me it is about job satisfaction.

Why do the charterers do it? There answer here is simple. The great thing about charterers is that they come with the intention of enjoying themselves: all you have to do is point them in the right direction and hang on to their oilskins. They also make you see things with fresh eyes. Simple things. I remember once we were hove-to for lunch, eight oil-skinned figures huddled in the cockpit, and one of the party suddenly burst out, 'This is fantastic, absolutely fantastic!' Surprised, I asked him why. 'Well, sitting here, reefed down, out of sight of land, eating ravioli, it's fantastic!' I suppose if you work regularly in an office block it could seem fantastic. It would definitely be a change from the canteen.

My boat is a 38ft yawl, and sleeps eight - seven of them and me, and between us we keep her going, winter and summer. There is always one who slips into the position of mate, but what is more important, there is invariably one at least whom I term 'fireproof'. Fireproof as regards seasickness. Give me every time the crewmate who, when you are two reefs down somewhere in the middle of the North Sea, pokes their head out of the hatch and asks, 'Soup, sandwiches or both, skip?'

Charterers, like me, enjoy change, in fact sometimes to a fault. They become so carried away with the novelty of a night passage that if you don't keep a check on them they won't wake up the next watch. Their invariable excuse is all noble and self-sacrificing ('We thought we'd let them have a good night's sleep') and not that they are enjoying themselves and, more to the point, not realising that watch-keeping is the method of keeping the boat sailing and all the crew rested.

I remember coming out of Sandwich one midnight with what turned out to be the ideal party for the circumstances: seven civil engineers. Someone had moved the channel and we went aground right on top of a spring tide. We turned in as there was nothing we could do right then, but at dawn we set to. We dug a trench, with oars and wooden shovels, for the boat to drop into, put out leading marks and lines to keep us in when we floated, dug a channel to the nearest gut (fortunately quite close), and more leading marks so that we knew when to turn into the main channel. When we floated, there was a spell of exciting dinghy work recovering anchors and lines – all good, interesting, seamanlike stuff. We headed for North

Foreland, the crew arguing that they should have a deduction for the work they had put in, and me saying that I should charge extra for laying on such a satisfactory excerpt. They booked again. I even have a beautiful little engraved brass plaque sent by one party, which is screwed to the beam shelf. There is a spelling mistake in it, as it says, 'To the skipper of *Grindstone*', but I'm sure they meant well; at least I think they did.

Years before I took up sailing, I was keen on mountains and, being hard up, used to work in the summer as a courier-cum-guide, taking people up mountains and making sure they didn't get lost or fall off. In those days many of the Alpine peaks had huge crucifixes on top with metal boxes on them in which were visitors' books where one wrote one's name and appropriate phrases. A favourite was, '*Desto nahe dem Himmel, desto ferne der Arbeit*' ('So near to Heaven, so far from work'). My parties liked this; they would copy it out, sign underneath and hand it to me to sign. 'But I'm not far from work. I'm working,' I'd say. None of them would believe me. It's the same now. Nobody believes it's true, only me, especially on a wet and windy Friday night.

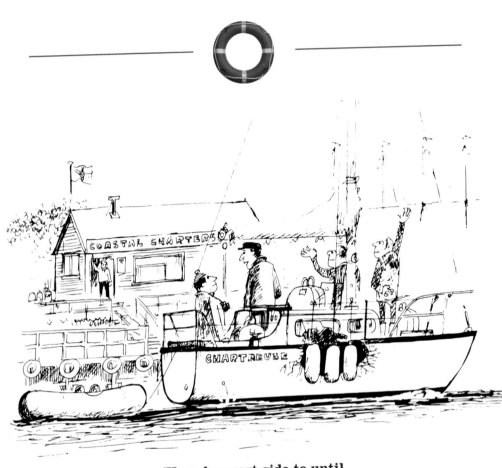

'Keep her port side to until
we get the deposit back.'

'Hold your course Dave.
We don't want to confuse him now!'

Chapter 5

One of those trips

The job in hand was simple. Danny and I sail together, and as we needed to make life easier for ourselves, we were faced with a decision – either a smaller boat or a bigger engine. My wife, who has seen three ferro boats (*Lodestone, Brimstone and Touchstone*) grown in the garden, was emphatic as to which is should be (*Tombstone* was even mentioned, not entirely in jest). So on 1st November, Danny and I set off to sail *Touchstone* from Maldon in Essex to the Humber, where Danny would install the larger engine. The boat would lie in the haven near his house at Wintringham and he would do it at his convenience. Also with us was Lorenzo, a Swiss boy of 16 who had been sent over (I quote his elder brother) 'to learn things in England he can't learn in Switzerland.' I don't think he ever appreciated how right he was.

It is about a 240-mile trip, and *Touchstone*, with three reefs in and an offshore wind, made good time through the night. Just short of Great Yarmouth, approximately the half-way mark, I made the fatal mistake of working out our ETA. As if on cue, we picked up a warning for a north-westerly gale, the last thing one wants when going into the Humber. So we went into Great Yarmouth instead and were almost alongside the mooring when we lost propulsion – a pin in the variable pitch prop had sheared.

We got alongside safely, but knew that this job would have to wait until next weekend.

It rained throughout the time it took to do the job and the tide complicated matters considerably but, to cut a long, long story short, the prop was dismantled and reassembled three times in two days. Lorenzo, or Lori to which he now answered, learned how to keep the fire going and to make tea and toast, as well as just about every swear word in the book, with a Yorkshire accent. Danny kept muttering about how it beat him why he didn't join the Over-Sixties Club.

But with prop propelling again, we didn't waste much time, and though the forecast wasn't too good, we knew that if it did blow up we had a weather shore to anchor off. A couple of miles east of Cromer we listened to the 1355 forecast and I shackled on the main anchor in case the southwesterly gale they forecast arrived. Our immediate plan was to try and get to Blakeney before it was too dark to see the unlit buoys that would lead us over the bar and into the anchorage beyond. That was some 18 miles away and we had less than three hours of daylight left. But with plenty of wind – we had two reefs in – and the engine going, and with calm water, we reckoned we would do it.

Then the sky ahead of us went black, simply solid black. Danny and I put our oilskins on and when the squall did hit, it was as if a powerful hose had been directed at us. I dowsed the jib and Danny the mizzen – his gammy leg generally keeps him in the cockpit. Lori, sensible lad, went below. I suppose – being his first day at sea – it was understandable. Days later I asked him what he found the greatest difference between England and Switzerland. He looked at me as if I was an idiot and replied, 'The sea, of course.'

When I got back to the cockpit Danny started on again about the attractions of the Over-Sixties Club. I had just come to the conclusion that there was no way we would see our way to Blakeney, when suddenly we saw daylight again. The squall had passed and the possibility of making it was there again.

The light had almost gone as I dropped the mainsail east of the offing buoy. We were surrounded by broken water; it was touch and go, to say the least, and we literally lived from buoy to buoy. But we made it into the deep water moorings and had a rare stroke of luck by finding a dan buoy marking a massive fishing boat mooring. It was doubled with two rope eyes lashed to it. We got on board, passed the dan buoy to Lori, made fast

31

and had just relaxed when we realised the buoy was no longer with us. We both looked at Lori. He looked into the darkness.

The dinghy was unlashed and launched in record time and off I went down wind and tide, where it would obviously be. So it was, but that was the easy bit. Getting back was a much harder job. The only sign of life was the distant masthead light which Danny had thoughtfully switched on. I ended up wading, towing the dinghy in shallow water well past that tiny spark of light, then getting in again and crabbing across the tide. I finally made it, just.

For the next couple of days the shipping forecasts always seemed to start with, 'Gale warnings in all areas except Trafalgar' and as time was running out, I decided that Wells would be a far more convenient place to make a start from the next time round, and we could leave the boat lying alongside.

The forecast was still for gales, but they weren't blowing at that moment, and surely we could manage five miles' motor-sailing with reefed main and an offshore wind? Bumpy is an understatement, but fortunately we didn't start touching until we were well in and in sheltered water. A local fisherman came out in his dinghy and led us in to the quay, where the Harbourmaster took our lines. He told us we were lucky and that he had switched off Channel 12 as he didn't expect anyone to be coming in so late. He said that no water flows out of Wells, it being a marsh harbour, and that it is very susceptible to the wind. We found this out the hard way.

The following morning I was in a London office, and I can assure you there is nothing more likely to put you off your work than to receive a phone call and be told that your boat has a 6ft hole in it.

Apparently what had happened was that the wind had gone round to the north and blown a gale, and the fetch on this part of the coast is from the North Pole. It was entirely unprotected, and the seas had come rolling into the harbour with waves breaking over the quay. The fenders had been washed out and *Touchstone* had crashed against the quay – the end result, the 6ft hole.

When I rejoined them, even though Danny had patched the hole with Expocrete (a plastic cement), *Touchstone* still showed the marks of her experience. Seaweed hung over the guardrails, flattened and burst fenders were still tied on, as were a couple of mattresses that had been pressed, literally, into service. Below, the carpet was wet. All the same, *Touchstone* was ready for sea, but the sea wasn't ready for us.

The wind had gone round to the south-west and there wasn't enough

'When I got back to the cockpit Danny started on again about
the attractions of the Over-Sixties Club.'

water over the bar. We couldn't get out until a couple of days later. The wind was ideal – Force 3 to 4 south-westerly; the only drawback was the visibility. There wasn't any. We felt our way through the fog with the last of the daylight to help. Half an hour later, for days are short in November, it was like being in the proverbial inside of a cow. We laid a course for Brancaster Roads some five miles away.

We were quite happy to let Lori stand a watch as he was a keen orienteer, so he knew the theory. After all, he was here to learn, although what good it was to him back home in Switzerland heaven only knows. Once in deep water we had a 10-mile slant to the north-west until we found three metres, where we anchored for the night and turned in until the next ebb. The alarm awoke me again in time to hear the 0555 forecast. It promised fives, sixes and perhaps a seven, south-westerly, but it didn't worry us. Somewhere out there in the murk was a weather shore.

We had breakfast and set off navigating by soundings, into three metres, out to five into three, out . . . and so on. Just as on the night before, it was a totally abstract problem, and it was very satisfying when we got a long westerly run which told us we had rounded the Haile Sands Flat. A bit of imaginative navigation came to naught when Danny thought he could smell the British Oil and Cake Mills, but I tracked it down to some mulligatawny soup burning on the stove. A short run north, and an hour and a half later we were ashore on the mud at the entrance to Wintringham Haven, waiting for the rapidly rising tide to lift us in.

It was Sunday, the last day of November, a month to the day since we set off. It was Lori who summed it up when, a few days later, a sailing friend of mine called at the house and asked what sort of a trip we had had. Lori answered in his best Yorkshire accent, 'It was a big of a boogar.'

PEYTON

'There's times, Peter, when I wish you
weren't such an enthusiast.'

Chapter **6**

In the peace of an evening

There is one thing you can expect on a boat, and that is the unexpected. Relax for a minute and there it is. And it's not on some hairy night passage that things happen; then you are, metaphorically speaking, on your toes. It's during the quiet times. I'll give you an example.

It had been an absolute gem of a summer's day and I got away early and went down to the mooring mid-week to potter. The yard was just finishing for the day as I arrived, so it must have been about five o'clock. Dick, the engineer, saw me and said he had been on board and taken the injectors off; 'I'll get it fixed by the weekend.' Coming over the sea wall I remember thinking, 'What a waste of a day – all these boats at their moorings, all their owners in stifling offices in town...'

It was idyllic, the water like glass, the sun still high and warm but not unpleasantly so. I rowed out and as I did so vaguely thought about the odd jobs I might do – first, paint the blade of one of the oars while the day was still warm. I could scull back. I had lost an oar and the new one still had a varnished blade while the other was painted red. I climbed on board and opened up the boat, then pulled up the dinghy and took out the new oar, wiped the blade and propped it up to dry while I dropped down the forehatch to get the paint. I found it, opened it, stirred it and came on deck. The dinghy had gone.

I knew what had happened. There had been a bowline on the end of the painter which I had simply dropped over a winch, and as I had eased myself back after getting the oar I had lifted it off. Now the dinghy was away on the tide. I was marooned – no wind, no engine, no one about to ask for help. I thought of drudging but, besides all those mooring chains to foil, by the very nature of things I would be travelling more slowly than the dinghy. I had got around to considering the long swim ashore with a lifebuoy when a breath of wind ruffled the water.

Headsail to bend on, sail cover off the main – I knew what to do now and I went at it like a mad thing. This is the wrong way to do things on a boat and I proved it by kicking over the tin of red paint. Moreover I walked a fair bit of it around the decks in my rush before I realised it. To say I was furious is an understatement. I picked up the tin and flung it as far as I could. It was another mistake – there was still some paint in it and as it hurtled away it left a trail of red paint in the air behind it. I watched it fall. Besides more on the deck I now had it on the sail and topside. As I have said, it was marvellous drying weather, so it was out turps and clean up immediately.

At the finishing of the cleaning-up operation the wind was still faint but fair so up went the sails and over went the mooring buoy. I was through the moorings and beyond when I happened to glance back. About four boats up in the centre trot was the dinghy. It was held against a boat by the painter being on one side of the buoy, snagged by the knot, and the dinghy itself on the other.

I now had to beat back against the last of the flood, but the wind was so fickle and faint that I could barely hold my own. In fact at times I couldn't, and I would have done better to put the kedge down. About one and a half hours later the tide turned and I gradually started making my way through the moorings. So did the dinghy.

By now my worry was that I would be carried through the moorings before I caught my dinghy, because the wind had now gone completely and I was making way by pulling my boat up past moored boats and pushing off towards the next one on the trot. I was dripping with sweat – my boat is a 10-tonner. Once I almost caught the dinghy when the mizzen boom caught in the backstay of a moored boat and held me back at the critical moment. I could have wept. My method was to try to get close enough to throw the lead across a thwart. When I finally got it I had actually done this and missed getting it inboard, but I hit the transom hard enough to send it one side of a moored boat as I was on the other. But I was waiting at the other end and managed to restrain myself from plunging the boat hook straight through the bottom. I then hauled and pushed my way through the moorings and when finally I got near my own I rowed out a line. I had grasped the buoy and was making the line fast when there was a puff of wind and she sheered across the tide. After the efforts I had gone through to get there I would have been torn in two rather than let go. But it was the last fitful kick. I got the mooring on board, climbed back into the dinghy and cleaned off the splotches of paint on the topsides – the ones I had missed when doing it from the deck. Then I got back on board and slumped in the cockpit. Recovering, I suppose, is the word.

It was almost three hours since I had first climbed on board. As I sat there I saw a figure appear on the sea wall. He stood there for a few minutes as I had done some three long hours earlier, taking in the peace of the evening. I watched him sourly, thinking, `You stupid idiot, why didn't you get down here earlier?' He slid his dinghy into the water, rowed out into the stream and drifted down on the tide.

`A marvellous evening', he called across as he drifted by, resting on his oars. I grunted in reply.

`What time did you get down?'

`About five.'

`Lucky devil.'

'You can't beat it, Tony. A good sail, a quiet drink,
then a row back in the moonlight to a snug little cabin . . .'

'John, would you go to Channel 72?
I want to ask you something.'

Chapter 7

Safe at anchor

There are many misnomers in sailing. Safe at anchor is one of them. Richard and myself had anchored *Touchstone* in the Upper Gull in the River Ore. We had foregone the delights of Aldeburgh, beer, and fish and chips, for the more aesthetic appeal of the fluting of the seabirds at the south end of the Gull. We had gone there for comfort and a more sheltered anchorage, with a forecast of Force 5–6s from the south-west.

We were as close as we dared to Havergate Island and, having done our sums to leave 1m of water under us at low water, we let go the anchor. Though windy, it was a warm July night, and sitting in the cockpit as dusk fell we were in a world that was pure Maurice Griffiths, except that our drinks were neither Oxo nor cocoa. A darkening world of wind and water. As befits such a world, the only other boat in the anchorage was a Thames sailing barge, wind rode against the ebb.

To the north-east we could see the regular flash of the Orfordness light and the no-man's land of mudbanks, between the dark tide and the saltings, literally covered with Canada geese. We seemed to be along way from anywhere.

We finished our drinks, put up the riding light and turned in, East Coast yotties content with their lot.

My wife has often told a slightly derogatory story about me and how, when the house was struck by lightning and the television set went up in flames, I slept through it all, yet – this is the punch line: 'Strike a match on the boat and he's up like a jack-in-the-box.'

I never say anything when this story is trotted out for, as many other yachtsmen can vouch, it's true that a skipper seems to get hyper-sensitive on board – although, in my case at least, only on my own boat. Unfortunately, the bell does not ring every time.

I awoke for what reason I know not. From the clock I could see it was 0400, about high water. I could see the glow of the riding light through the forehatch. It was quiet, except for the wind, which was still blowing, and all seemed well, but from past experience I knew I had to get up. As I went through the hatch I knew immediately what had happened. The wind had gone round and we were no longer laid off the shore, but lying stern in with the boat out at an angle. I tried the rudder. No movement. I switched on the echo sounder. The transducer is just forward of the mast and it gave 3m.

I was wide awake now. I pressed the starter button and 'Perkins' sprang into life. Within seconds Richard was coming through the hatch. He took the situation in at a glance and without a word went forward and started hauling – winching was too slow – to take the slack on the anchor chain.

That's sailing for you. One minute in the land of dreams, the next hauling desperately on mud-covered ⅜in anchor chain in your Y-fronts, adrenalin in full flood.

Luck was with us and we came off. We could have relaid the anchor and gone back to our still warm bunks, but I did not have to tell Richard what I was thinking. We have sailed a lot together and he has his own boat. He realised, as I did, that the windshift that had nearly ruined our day was, through shifting, now a fair offshore wind down the coast. Dawn was just breaking, and by the time we got to the entrance of the river we would have enough light to see the leading marks to guide us over the bar. It was so obvious. He handed me a coat from the doghouse as he went below to clean up and dress. By the time we reached the river's entrance, we were dressed, decks sluiced, the anchor lashed and stowed. We had even had a coffee, and to all intents and purposes we were ready for sea with the day – a long day at that – before us. All because I had been so unseamanlike as not to allow myself swinging room.

The only occasion – and this is historical – when it would have paid not to have allowed swinging room was for the French Admiral Brueys at the Battle of the Nile. He had prepared for an expected meeting with Nelson by anchoring his fleet fore and aft, parallel to a line of shoals off the coast, and moved some of the guns pointing inshore to face out to sea. When the British fleet arrived with a commanding wind, Nelson reasoned that no seaman worth his salt would anchor so close inshore that he had not got swinging room. So he split his fleet and sailed down both sides of the French line. I have often wondered what the hapless Brueys thought as the realisation dawned at the time.

Once over the bar, with a fair wind and everything set and drawing, I went below to cook breakfast, and as I did so I mused, as I often do, on the ups and downs of sailing. Was it only an hour ago we were asleep in our bunks? Then as I turned over the bacon I thought about what could have happened. Suppose I reacted to television sets instead of boats? I shuddered at the thought.

'There are times I wish I'd never
read Maurice Griffiths.'

Chapter 8

Down with fitting out

Fitting out is all things to all men. I know people, and I have no doubt you do too, who fit out constantly from one laying up day to the next one, 12 months later. That is how they get their pleasure and good luck to them. They have got it made.

But I'm not keen on fitting out. Boats, to my way of thinking, are for sailing in, not working on, and I have devoted a lot of thought to how to avoid fitting out.

The Victorians obviously had the answer: paid hands. I have often thought how pleasant it would have been to have sailed in those distant days if it wasn't for the nagging doubt that I would probably have been the paid hand.

Once you have started thinking about doing away with fitting out, or at least keeping it down to manageable proportions, a lot of obvious ideas spring to mind.

Stainless steel is one idea and, if you can afford it, it must pay off over the years in the way of stainless rigging, bottle screws, pushpits etc. Alloy spars are another time saver – admitted varnished ones look more nautical but masts are for pulling sails up, not sanding down. Any gear you can do without, do without.

Everything that goes on a boat needs some time spent on it and these suggestions are just scratching the surface, but anyone who has had a boat long enough to fit it out can tell you more.

What you have to do is to look at the problem in a much wider sense. Ask yourself the question, 'Why do I fit out?' The answer is because you laid up. The problem is solved. Don't lay up and you won't have to fit out. It is as simple as that.

Commercial craft do not lay up. Fitting out, if you can call it that for them, is a constant process to keep the boat shipshape and seaworthy. Modern materials and marinas lend themselves to this method of keeping a yacht or powerboat fitted out and ready for sea.

A present day GRP cruiser tied up in a marina or a mudberth with alloy spars, stainless rigging, synthetic sails with a good sail cover and an engine and electrics that get a regular spray of some moisture repellent gives you the best of both worlds. You go when the going is good, and work when south cones are hoisted.

British weather isn't geared up to set periods for fitting out and laying up. Statistically the traditional months for fitting out are among the windiest and wettest of the year. Winter months, on the other hand, can often offer you some good sailing days, even if they are a bit on the short side.

The long evenings when you are tucked away in some sheltered anchorage you can spend doing jobs below. Besides your tools you must also carry paint, varnish and brushes on board. You can get more painting done and a better job made of it in a couple of hours on a warm windless day in June than in a month of wet weekends in the winter.

Good painting and varnishing weather is when you are wearing shorts and sunglasses, preferably in some foreign harbour.

Spreading the load is another method of doing away with fitting out. You get volunteers down to do a weekend's work in return for a weekend's sailing. To look at it dispassionately as a time and motion exercise, if two people help you over one weekend then they and you are going to do more work in one weekend than you yourself will do in two. If three people help you the gain is all yours. So you work one weekend and sail the next with an easy conscience. If you give them a good sail they will probably sign on again.

If you get people down to work for you, try to ensure that the work programme is mapped out beforehand and all the tools and materials are ready and at hand so that they can get on with the job. If they have to wander off to get some screws, buy timber or wash paint brushes then it's your fault, not theirs.

Another habit that is worthwhile cultivating in keeping fitting out to the minimum is to do jobs as they occur through the season as quickly as possible.

It's bad policy to say, `I will leave it until I lay up'. Keeping a boat ready for sea is a constant process. The point to remember is that the boat is there to give you pleasure and if your pleasure comes from sailing it, you must concentrate all your effort and energy on keeping it seaworthy.

The cussedness of life is such that the more a boat is used, the more work needs doing to it and conversely, the less it is used, the less attention it needs but the more it seems to get.

One friend avoided fitting out for a number of seasons. His method was simple and unique and he still got his sailing in. All he did was to sell his boat at the end of the season and buy new at the beginning of the next one.

ever wonder why we do it?

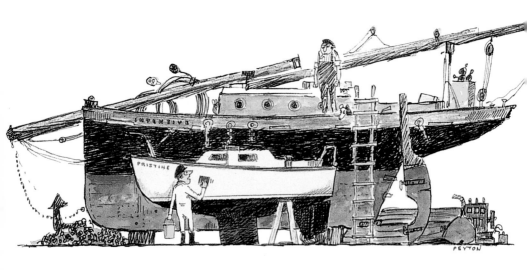

**'I don't know about you,
but I've a work list as long as my arm.'**

'I've no idea why they do it but it's always
in the small hours in their Y-fronts.'

Chapter 9

Over and out

I have only had one man-overboard for real. Fortunately, I got him back quite quickly and, though I have never read of the method I used being tried before, it just seemed the right thing to do in the circumstances. And it worked.

Since I ran my boat as a charter yacht, I was conscious of the man-overboard problem and the normal method of simulating it – a bucket tied to a fender – went over the side often enough.

Picking up a mooring was also treated as a man-overboard drill, as was retrieving anything that went over the side. This had the advantage that no one knew when it was going to happen. The thing recovered the most was hats, but we did rescue a five pound note once on the blade of an oar. I considered that that was close enough as the note was mine. Against that we lost a bobble hat in the Wallet Spitway because it was low water and we hadn't enough searoom to operate. Nevertheless, treating everything that went overboard as an excuse for a practice is a good method because it was invariably unexpected and in varying conditions.

But when it came to put what we had practised into use for the real thing, it all went out of the window. Even the engine was forgotten. I had a crowd of regulars on board: six rugby players. John, the one who went over the side, was about 102kg (16 stone). It happened in a second and it was surprising how quickly someone in the water is left behind.

There was a fresh wind blowing and I came back to him hove-to and fore-reaching slowly. We ended up with John grasping the base of a stanchion, just forward of the cockpit. Incongruously, he still had his pipe in his mouth. We had plenty of muscle on board but we couldn't concentrate it where it was needed.

It was then that the penny dropped. Unless I was in a hurry, I invariably towed a dinghy. I never thought of it as a drag, but as a safety precaution. It was a rigid plywood dinghy and I pulled it up past John until I could tie the painter to the shrouds. In this position John could get his arm in it. I then cast off the headsail sheet, sheeted it in on the other side and started sailing the boat. It was so obvious.

Immediately the boat started sailing, his legs trailed out behind him and the dinghy pressed into him. As the boat heeled, he was easily lifted out of the water by the hull, allowing him to get first one knee and then the other into the dinghy. I eased the sheets and he climbed back on board. It took literally minutes from the time he went overboard to the welcoming 'You stupid bast . . .'

I would hate to go out on a limb and say this is the way to do it because the permutations must be infinite – sea state, size of boat, type of person, weather, etc. But in this case, in the prevailing conditions, it worked. The wind and the boat provided the power and the lift we needed. It was effortless. I think I even got a drink out of it.

'Bloke hanging on the bobstay Fred,
wants to know the name of your insurance.'

'You should see land in an hour's time.'

Chapter 10

Solo act

There is a lot of truth in the saying that your good deeds are written in water and your bad deeds scratched on brass. Make a nonsense of something on a boat and the world and his wife will be on the quayside to watch you. Do something you are proud of and you will be lucky if you rate a second glance from a passing seagull.

However, I did help to redress the balance once as an appreciative audience of one. It was in Ramsgate; I was on a mooring. It was early morning and I had just put my head through the hatch to see what the day had to offer. There wasn't a soul in sight but as I glanced around the harbour I saw from the harbour signals that a boat was due.

I watched the entrance and a small Belgian yacht sailed in. There was one man on board; a single-hander at the end of a night passage. His preparations for entering the harbour were straight out of the book – fenders out both sides, warps ready, anchor and boathook handy and courtesy flag fluttering. He came in, summed up the situation – the moorings were all occupied – and saw where he had to go. The boats alongside the wall were three deep except in one place where there were only two abreast. It was near a ladder, but the space was very tight.

He shaped up for it and everything went like a dream. He timed the dropping of his sails to the second, was back at the tiller to wriggle his boat into the gap and his ship carried its way to the absolute inch. It stopped as the fenders kissed the side of the inside boat, and he made fast. It was perfect. Only then could he relax and see if he had the audience he deserved for his *tour de force*.

He looked around the harbour – not a soul moved. I had to do something, so I clasped my hands together as a boxer does when celebrating a victory and waved them above my head to show my appreciation. The movement caught his eye and he considered me across the harbour, his sole but appreciative audience.

I will always remember his reaction. Slowly and deliberately he stepped on to the cabin top, turned and faced me and stood stiffly to attention. Then with a graceful flourish of one hand, he gave a deep bow.

PEYTON

'Have I failed?'

'Don't you know? Four Fastnets, a Yachtmaster Examiner and
a City and Guilds in boatbuilding. She makes me sick.'

Chapter 11

Meanwhile, back at the yard

Twelve of us got together to buy the yard when it went broke. And, as yards go, it can be described as one of character. We often get yachtsmen wandering around taking in the atmosphere of the old wooden sheds and the boats chocked up at impossible angles. The yard is on a slope which runs down to the river. They'll pick their way carefully along the spidery jetties that go over the saltings, and if you speak to them they'll talk with nostalgia of how all this reminds them of the good old days. But they, of course, keep their boat in a marina.

However, it suits us. After all, we're only there for the moorings. Definitely not for the money; our rates are the cheapest on the river and financially we just tick over. If we charged more we would have to provide more. But being 'them' instead of 'us' does give a different viewpoint, mainly because, if nothing else, the yard has got to pay its own way. The sordid subject of money raises its ugly head. It can be summed up in a phrase known to every yachtsman – yard bills.

To give a couple of examples: when we first took over the yard, new brooms and all that, we found that there were four boats that hadn't been billed for years. Two of the owners we never did find and the boats had been there so long that when we tried to move them they fell apart, so we burnt them. This gave rise to a rumour that if you didn't pay your bills we burnt your boat. However, the other two owners were located. They had just been forgotten. And what a temptation!

For some time we had the wheel of a road trailer in the office. This was the direct result of a yard bill. We arrived at the yard one morning and someone had obviously tried to move one of the boats during the night. He had tried hard but he hadn't been able to move it as far as he wanted, which we surmised was over the hill and far away. The boat was in an awkward corner – the yard is full of them – and you didn't need to be Kojak to read the signs: the boat on its trailer, half-slewed out of its position; the hole in the raw earth where the wheels of the towing vehicle had spun fruitlessly. We even guessed the motive – a large outstanding bill.

I told this tale to someone in another boatyard and he pointed to a propeller in the corner of his office. In his case, the boat had been in a mudberth and they had arrived at the yard to find the boat aground on the mud but well out of its berth. Fortunately, it had been a windless night.

Obviously, when a boat is afloat, it is not so easy to keep a check on such customers. We had a couple at the yard who were living on board. This isn't supposed to happen, but we felt sympathetic and the DHSS couldn't provide them with accommodation ashore, so a blind eye was turned. The DHSS even paid their mooring fees – the only complaint we had was that they never passed them on to us. We heard later that they had spoken in the local of going to Holland because the Social Security benefits were better there. And go they did, on a midnight tide.

One client we still remember (though it is some years ago now) rang up requesting that his boat be launched on a bank holiday weekend. We mentioned what was then a fairly large outstanding bill. 'My cheque is in the post,' was the indignant reply, and so it was. In fact, the Post Office excelled itself and so did the bank, for not only did it arrive far quicker than the owner intended but the bank processed it fast enough for them to bounce it back to us the day before the four-day bank holiday weekend started. Fortunately for us, this owner had brought some friends with him as crew and we managed to get a £50 cheque off each one of them before we launched the boat. We lost a few pounds but considered ourselves lucky to get rid of him so cheaply.

Another client was also involved with the postal services, but in this case they were not at their best and the letter took about a week to arrive.

It was from an owner who had left the yard about 18 months previously. While the boat had been there we had installed a new engine for him, and it was this he was complaining about – he considered something we had done constituted a fire risk. We thought this an odd letter especially as only two days previously the boat in question had caught fire and sunk in deep water, a total wreck. The owner had rowed ashore in the flat calm that was then prevailing. The penny dropped when we received a letter from an insurance company who stated that a client was saying we had installed an engine for him and he had complained to us by letter that he considered it a fire risk. We replied saying that it was true he had written to us, but felt we should point out that the letter had been written 18 months after the engine had been installed and that it had arrived two days after the boat in question had caught fire and sunk. Even the most generous of us had doubts as to his honesty.

At the other end of the scale we have a man who pays on the nail and no one in the yard has ever seen him. The ideal customer? Perhaps the ideal customer would be a combination of him and another gentleman who limped into the office one afternoon nursing his knee to tell us what he thought about the bl... yard, and in particular one of the planks across our spidery jetties which had given way underneath him. Visions of us being sued ran through our minds as we waited silently for his tirade to finish, but we had misjudged him. He had actually come for a piece of timber and nails, which we willingly supplied to him, to repair the offending jetty.

Another customer works, or worked, somewhere in the Middle East and normally, when he received his first quarterly bill, he would send a cheque to cover the entire year. Consequently, he was always in credit. Then one year there was no reply, no cheque. We waited quite a long time before sending him a reminder. Still no reply to that and the others we sent. Now we are worried that his bones may be bleaching in some lonely desert wadi.

We had another client who disappeared and we only found out about this when the authorities contacted us asking if we could give them any information about him. They had got our address from opening the reminders we had sent him. Apparently his house had been found with the front door unlocked, the back door wide open and a half-eaten meal on the table. It was like the *Marie Celeste*. Both he and his wife had disappeared off the face of the earth.

Obviously not all our customers are in the same category as those mentioned above. We'd be in a bad way if they were. And the actions of this minority have been spread over the years. But I assure you we've had them, and I will lay odds that every boatyard and marina can cap these stories.

So if, in your wanderings around the shores of Britain, you get quizzical looks when, after tying up, you go to make your number at the office, you will realise that the boatyard is probably trying to work out if you are one of the ninety-nine per cent who are normal or one of the one per cent who aren't.

'I love wandering around these old boatyar . . .'

ever wonder why we do it?

'If they hadn't kept on about a measly yard bill,
we wouldn't have to leave like this.'

Chapter 12

Rediscovering Duff

Whenever one reads the reminiscences of the old-time bargemen, there always seems to be some mention of a duff constantly boiling its way to its destiny, which was to arrive hot and steaming on some bargeman's plate. There came a day when I felt I had to make one. It was, after all, my type of yacht cooking: running an eight-berth charter boat where the basic requirements of the meals can be summed up by the words 'tasty bulk'. A duff would fill them to the letter: traditional 'get that across your chest' fare.

Research told me that duffs came about by cooks trying to make the best of a bad job. Hard tack was normal fare in those distant days and, to try and make it more user-friendly, it was pounded up to powder, to which was added water and anything else that the cook fancied under the two headings: sweet or savoury. Once that decision was made, the mixture was wrapped in a cloth and boiled for a couple of hours. From all accounts it went down like an anchor, stuck to your ribs and altered your point of balance. Obviously I had to make one.

And so I did. It was slightly more up-market than the bargemen's, being culled from Mrs Beeton. The mixture was two of flour to one of suet with baking powder added, but in these days of self-raising flour the latter is now obsolete. The stiff, sticky lump was then put in a cloth which had been previously scalded and dredged on the inside with flour, which acted as a seal. The cloth was then tied up with string and boiled for a couple of hours.

But here I must make a confession. I mixed it at home, and it wasn't quite so basic as a traditional one. However, it now seems to me that anything goes and this was my recipe: flour, breadcrumbs, suet, mixed fruit, sugar, ginger and spices, all mixed together dry, and milk added to get a stiff sticky lump. Put it in a bowl and cover with greaseproof paper; this is to keep the condensation off it so it comes up relatively dry. You keep this in place with a rubber band or some light line, the latter being my favourite, as it allows you to put loops in it so that you can lift it out of the pan. Wrap it up in a cloth and boil it for at least two hours. From experience I now realise that the weights, after the basic two to one of flour and suet, are entirely up to the cook and the first one I made was with four people in mind.

The day we had might have been designed for a duff. It was mid-November and we had sailed from Maldon to the Stour and anchored just up from Wrabness. When we awoke in the morning, the fog that had been forecast had arrived in no mean manner. It was dense. Later in the morning we found our way by echo sounder to the old barge quay off Ewarton, where we anchored, built up the fire (my boat has a solid fuel stove with a fiddle) and, leaving the duff boiling away, rowed ashore and walked over the fields to The Queen's Head.

The plan was that, on our return, we would make a stew with the duff for afters, but it was not to be. We could smell the duff as we rowed back to the boat; in fact we could have homed in on it. Down below, the aroma was the duff's undoing. We decided unanimously to do the duff in first. It was unwrapped, divided, covered in syrup and devoured.

We never got around to a main course, nor did we need it. They knew a thing or two, those old bargemen.

PEYTON

'Keep her on this tack, skip,
until I serve the soup.'

Chapter 13

If a job's worth doing . . .

Sometimes you just know a job is not going to go as it should and invariably you get a warning. I got mine immediately and if I had had any sense I would have gone home there and then and done some of the jobs my wife is always asking me to do instead.

The job was simple enough. My boat has a rubbing band with a sacrificial layer of ply as an outer skin. A five foot section near the bows had been damaged and I needed to replace it. I had put the boat in a mudberth to do the job but owing to North Easterlies that had been blowing and a slack line, she wasn't sitting fair in it. I hauled the dinghy over the mud from the stern and made it fast to the pulpit and then, making sure everything I needed in the way of tools was accessible on the foredeck, I climbed over the pulpit and lowered myself down. I hung there for a few seconds at full stretch with my nose rubbing against the hull and my toes feeling for the side of the dinghy. They made contact, I let go and as my weight came down, the dinghy slid aside and I ended up in the mud to my knees. I struggled out to the sea wall and it was then I should have gone home. It was going to be one of those jobs.

I went along to the tap to clean up, got back on board and repositioned the dinghy by a dint of manhandling with boat hook and painter, climbed over the pulpit and lowered myself down. I dangled there again with my nose rubbing the hull, then let go and landed fair in the dinghy.

Now I could start.

I offered up the piece of ply: it only needed about an inch off. I sawed it off and offered it up again. It wouldn't quite fit – too little to saw; too much to go in.

All I needed was Surform.

The Surform was in the tool locker.

Getting back on board was a struggle: stand on side of dinghy, grasp leg of pulpit, hand over hand to bottom rail, good grasp, heave, grunt, strain, struggle, make it.

Warm.

Took off coat and hung it on cleat on the mast.

Got Surform.

Over pulpit.

Dangle, rub nose, drop, take off smidge of wood.

Perfect fit.

Drill holes, countersink – where are screws?

In coat pocket.

Where is coat?

Hanging on the cleat on the mast.

I considered struggling through the mud and walking along to the tap but decided to climb.

Hand over hand, strain, strive, struggle, make it.

Get screws and go below to get extra ones just in case: over pulpit, dangle, drop. Have got four screws in when a thought strikes me.

I sit on a thwart to consider.

This piece of ply I am screwing on has an end grain which is going to disappear from human eyes for ever. It should have a coat of something on it. Obviously I would varnish the ply to match in with the rest. That could be done from the deck when the job is finished, but the end grain . . . I unscrew the screws, place the ply across the thwarts, grasp, grunt, heave, strain, struggle make it.

I get the varnish and go for the brush.

Bear with me in the following. The varnish brush is kept in a tin of white spirits under the chart table seat. Normally it is jammed alongside the box that holds the log. The last trip the boat had done had been to

Calais in fog and the log had been used. The boat had heeled. With no box to restrain it, the tin had fallen over and the brush had slipped between the bottom of the locker and the hull. I looked underneath. It had also slipped between the cabin sole and the hull – it was in the bilges.

In the general course of events I would have simply lifted up the floor-boards – but not this time. A few days earlier I had made an extra step down into the cabin and although screwed down it was, in a manner of speaking, on probation. If it worked, the floorboards would be cut to suit; in the meantime the floorboards were fixed and I needed a screwdriver to get them up.

It was in the dinghy.

I went to get it.

Over the pulpit, dangle, drop, screwdriver, grasp, grunt, heave, struggle, strain. Back on board, I dismantle the step and take up the floorboards.

In getting the boards up, a corner of the carpet I have on the cabin sole jammed. I gave it a pull (or, to be honest, I grabbed it and gave it a wrench). It tore right down the middle.

Coldly and dispassionately, I found the brush, cleaned it, got the varnish and went back to the pulpit. Taking a firm grasp of myself I considered what needed to be done and what I would need to do it. Mentally I checked and re-checked and came to the conclusion that there was nothing, absolutely nothing, that could prevent me finishing that simple job. I climbed over the pulpit, dangled and dropped.

Now, as time has softened the impact, I can stand the memory – but in that final drop I landed on the ply which was resting across the thwarts. It nearly broke me, let alone the ply.

ever wonder why we do it?

'I've noticed it after every boat show –
a certain discontent with their lot.'

'Between you and me, I don't think
the boat show is our scene.'

Chapter 14

Following your nose

I recently read an article in my local newspaper with deep interest and I have no doubt other local yachtsmen read it in the same way. It stated that the sewer outfall had been extended. Not a world-shattering piece of news, admitted, but as a navigational aid in bad visibility the sewage outfall is a winner. Not only can you hear the gulls that invariably cluster around it but you can *smell* it. There are times when you can be quite some way off it when you pick up signs of its discharge and you simply have to follow the trail back to its source. And there you are at a known point, which as the local paper informs me, is now two hundred yards further seaward.

All this is covered by the term `Barking Dog Navigation' (BDN), which in my experience mainly seems to be associated with fog. I once sailed with a fisherman who quite literally used a barking dog to navigate back to his berth. His dog barked whenever he appeared at the mouth of the creek irrespective of the weather – just as a buoy flashes night and day. When the weather was thick and he was creeping up the river he would stick his head out of the wheelhouse, turn into the creek and home in to his berth with an easy conscience.

I will always remember one foggy winter's night when two of us were feeling our way up the Kentish shore and we got this indication of land. I looked at my companion; he nodded. It was faint but definite and unmis-takable – fish and chips. We turned into the wind and shortly afterwards the lights on the harbour heads of Whitstable appeared.

Later that evening I remember my companion standing on the harbour wall after we had visited the fish and chip shop holding his supper above his head. His reply to my query was `Lengthening the range in case there is anyone else out there.'

As can be appreciated, this sort of navigation must be used with care; in this specific case one might even say take it with a pinch of salt. The more so since fish and chip shops have nights off. When using BDN the prudent skipper must be sensible – the hum of a power station would be pretty safe – after all, they are not too plentiful. But I remember once hearing some music when we were feeling our way down the coast in fog. I too readily assumed it was from a pier because it was that sort of music and, probably more to the point, it fitted in with my estimated position. A Doubting Thomas on board switched on the radio and soon found the same music. We then realised that there was a fishing party anchored in the vicinity. So obviously each one has to be taken on its merits.

But I think I can rely on the sewage outfall. Once I remember a crew member showing his confidence in it with a contradiction in terms. He called back from the bows, `It's okay we're in the sh ...'

PEYTON

ever wonder why we do it?

'I've just called the marina with our ETA.'

Chapter 15

Beware the zimmer frame of mind

When you get past your biblical sell-by date, like me, I can assure you that your sailing activities will alter. And if you say, `That doesn't affect me,' – worry not – it will someday. I can also assure you that the old adage of one foot of waterline length for every year of age is nonsense. I would say four inches to a year of age is a better parameter, unless you have a paid hand or two.

The *main* thing to avoid is the zimmer frame of mind and as you approach top dead centre in your sailing life the size of your boat is a critical factor. A small boat can be too lively for legs that have lost their spring, whereas a larger boat may have gear that is too heavy for arms that have lost their strength. Somewhere, there is probably an equation of how many aspirins a week as against water line length. (For the uninitiated, aspirins are a standard issue by the NHS after you reach your sell-by date.)

Of course all problems about size can be solved if you get a regular crew. Ideally, if you are male, she should be at least thirty years younger than you, fit and active and with a true appreciation of the experience and maturity that only comes with age. But failing that, almost anyone will do. I have had a one-armed man and I have even had someone older than myself (and there are not a lot of them about). In fact, some years ago when we were much younger, two of us sailed around England together with a combined age of 155, though that is of naught when compared to the three on board Ben Pester's *Marelle*. His crew's age totalled 193, but then they did go round Cape Horn. I must stress that one should make the most of sailing when you can. The reason I say this is that for years I took out charter parties on a regular basis – invariably there were six or seven of them – and those that are left still come. The last bunch of regulars I took out were the survivors and there were three of them. So sail while you can!

However there are a few basics. Watch the weather forecast. You have nothing to prove. If you decide to stay local it needn't be too local. I thoroughly recommend a (clockwise) trip around England, and it also allows one to get the full benefit of the geriatric's railcard. A good engine that starts on the button and good ground tackle are handy, as the days of cavorting on the foredeck at night in your Y-fronts are long past. Now I no longer have charter parties to keep occupied with hauling up the anchor, I recommend most emphatically a winch. I have also found a rowing machine bought at a car boot sale very useful. I have it sited in front of the TV and use it as I watch the news every night. As you can imagine, the spin off with regards to dinghy work (I have a rigid dinghy) is invaluable. I have also convinced myself that the strengthened stomach muscles allow my bladder to see me through the night, or almost.

But as mentioned previously, the main thing is to avoid the zimmer frame of mind.

'Best thing I ever did was to sell the boat
and become a social member.'

ever wonder why we do it?

'Have you ever stopped to analyse
what we're doing?'

Chapter 16

Christmas presents past

I am ashamed to admit this but a few years ago I put a bit of a dampener on the Peyton family Christmas by my own complete lack of imagination. I was unwrapping a Christmas present – a book on butterflies – when according to my wife (who has a tendency to exaggerate) I bellowed: 'Does no one in this house realise I am keen on sailing?'

The present was from my youngest daughter who, you may have guessed, was keen on butterflies. The Christmas spirit finally prevailed and all was well but the penny had dropped and as next Christmas approached I realised things had altered. I also realised, or was made to realise, that what is good for the goose is good for the gander. If pairs of socks were not good enough for me, gift tokens for Boots were no good for them.

Since that Christmas I have had some marvellous festive presents. I can see one now as I write and I use it daily: a wind vane on the garage roof. And what makes it special is that it has a silhouette of my boat on it. I've had a set of fenders – even gift-wrapped, I recognised them for what they were under the tree. Another Christmas it was a span of 10mm chain and a reel of rope. I've also had a pair of sheet winches – second-hand admittedly – but who cares?

My wife now asks my sailing friends for ideas and when a regular crewmember suggested a spinnaker, she was all in favour until she found out the price. `He's not worth that!' she exclaimed. However, the friend was quick-witted enough to suggest a second-hand spinnaker and even now he will say, when conditions are favourable, `I reckon she'll carry the Christmas present.'

But as the more discerning amongst you will have realised, this arrangement is a double-edged sword. One has to repay in kind. And I can assure you one has to be constantly on the lookout for ideas.

One extremely successful present only cost me a phone call. It happened when I found out purely by chance that place names on Ordnance Survey maps are generally arrived at by local usage. I rang up the Ordnance Survey and told them that a small wood my wife had planted was now known as Kath's Wood. They came down to check and it is now on the OS maps. They sent me a copy which I gift-wrapped and put under the tree.

A more expensive idea was six one-to-one Spanish lessons. I say more expensive, as my wife enjoyed them so much she kept on with them.

You win some, you lose some! Another ultimately successful idea cost almost nothing but there was a rather serious drawback. My wife was keen on riding and as she was getting older and stiffer, she was finding it difficult to mount her old mare. I got the idea of making her a concrete mounting block – for one who has built three ferro sailing boats this was no big problem. In fact the biggest problem was getting it into position on Christmas Eve without her seeing it, as it took two people to manhandle and wasn't the sort of present one could gift-wrap and put under the Christmas tree.

Come Christmas morning, when her queries came as to the where-abouts of her Christmas present, I told her it was about and she would find it sooner or later. Which of course she did – the only snag was she was reversing the car at the time and a block of concrete approximately two feet by two hasn't much give in it. The Christmas spirit was stretched for a time, I must admit.

PEYTON

'Yes, I'm quiet, and yes I'm thinking. I'll tell you
what about when we get the children to bed.'

Chapter 17

Last sail of the season

Our first `Christmas sail' started as many good things do – over a drink. It was at a party and half a dozen of us, yachtsmen all, lulled by the warmth, jollity and drink, agreed it would be a good idea to embark upon a day's sail on the most favourable tide nearest Christmas. Out in the morning and back in the evening.

Soon, the idea had taken on a life of its own. We were to have a turkey – cold, admittedly – with the trimmings cooked on board. I heard snippets of planning on the phone: `If you do the turkey I'll do the Christmas pudding and mince pies. Pam's doing the soup and veg.' As it was my boat, I was detailed to decorate the cabin. And so it went on.

The day duly dawned. The wind was howling past the chimney pots and the rain lashed at the windows; it was mid-December after all. Eight of us and a dog mustered on the sea wall at Fambridge on the River Crouch in Essex and so much food and drink went below I wondered if the boat would lift on the tide to get out of her berth. We reefed the main and bent on the small headsail as we waited for two latecomers. My heart sank as I saw them appear: they had a carrycot between them. `Sorry, the babysitter has let us down.'

That is how I date that trip, some 35 years ago, as the then occupant of the carrycot now has a family of his own and we have aged with him. The average age of last year's jaunt was 60-plus.

On that distant first day we roared down the empty River Crouch: *Lodestone* heeled to the wind and got down to it. Cold and bleak as it was, I was not the only muffled figure in the cockpit who wished the river had been longer, for it was a magnificent sail. We rounded up by Shore Ends, ran her into the bank at low water in the shelter of Foulness and retired below to our turkey and trimmings. The chimney blazed and the cups overflowed with mulled wine. Someone even came up with a Christmas riddle – Q. What has twenty-eight legs, two wings and an anchor? A. Eleven people and a dog eating turkey on *Lodestone*. You can see what mulled wine does to the intellect. Below there was warmth and light, the murmur of voices and laughter. About me was approaching night and a dark tide barely reflecting the last vestige of daylight and the first stars as it flooded across the mudflats. Tides as old as time yet always new. How many yachtsmen must have leaned in a hatchway as I was doing and marvelled at the fantastic contrast of his dark, cold, watery playground and the tiny capsule of comfort which floated on it? I went below to warm mince pies and more mulled wine.

Since that first year, we have experienced everything the seasonal weather has to offer, from drifting back on the tide to a full gale. We sailed once with a gale forecast and ran down the Blackwater under staysail alone, estimating we would be tied up in Bradwell Marina before the wind arrived in force. We did, but when the time came to leave, the wind was still howling and the marina was a cacophony of shrieking rigging and rattling halyards. Home bases were called for transport and the crew departed.

Only Peter and I stayed behind to get the boat back when the wind eased. We had a pleasant evening yarning with the odd drink or two and then turned in. We were awakened in the small hours by the sound of silence – no howling wind, shrieking rigging or rattling halyards – just silence. A glance through the hatch and we saw stars; a glance at the clock, and no words were needed. The tide served and with a light fair wind, we sailed up the deserted river under a frosty sky singing carols. We thought we sounded marvellous – it may have been the mulled wine – but either way it had been a perfect sail and we have done it every Christmas since.

'Perhaps it's not such a good idea.'

'My wife reckons sailing is sordid!'

ever wonder why we do it?